The New Guide To Guide To Mastering Canva

The Essential Handbook to Creating Stunning Designs for Every Purpose

ASHER M. BROOKS

the written permission of the publisher.

TABLE OF CONTENT

The New Guide To Mastering Canva

Preface

Welcome to *Mastering Canva: The Ultimate Guide to Visual Creativity*. This book is your comprehensive companion to understanding, using, and ultimately mastering Canva—a tool that has redefined how we approach design and creativity. Whether you're a beginner eager to create your first digital masterpiece or a seasoned designer looking to streamline your workflow, this book is crafted with you in mind.

About This Book

This guide is more than just a technical manual; it's a journey into the world of creative design powered by Canva. Its purpose is to demystify the platform's features—from its extensive template library and intuitive drag-and-drop interface to its groundbreaking AI tools like Magic Studio. Within these pages, you will discover:

- **A Clear Roadmap:** Step-by-step instructions to build your design skills, starting with the basics and progressing to advanced techniques.
- **Practical Exercises:** Hands-on projects and challenges that allow you to immediately apply what you learn.
- **Real-World Applications:** Insights on using Canva for various purposes such as social media marketing, branding, education, and digital product creation.
- **Additional Resources:** Curated links, community forums, and further reading recommendations to deepen your learning.

The target audience ranges from creative entrepreneurs and business owners to educators and hobbyists—anyone who wants to transform ideas into visually stunning realities. By blending theory with practice, this book serves as a definitive resource to unlock your full creative potential using Canva.

My Canva Journey

I still remember the moment I first stumbled upon Canva—an intimidating design task had me browsing for an accessible solution. I was overwhelmed by traditional design software, but Canva's intuitive interface and vibrant community quickly turned that challenge into a delightful exploration of creativity.

In my early days, I used Canva to design simple social media posts and event flyers. With each project, I discovered new features that sparked my imagination. The ease of dragging and dropping elements, the instant access to high-quality templates, and the revolutionary AI tools like Magic Design and Magic Edit transformed how I approached every creative project.

This journey wasn't just about learning a tool—it was about changing my entire outlook on design. I learned that creativity isn't reserved for professional designers; it's a universal language accessible to all. Through trial, error, and countless moments of inspiration, Canva helped me express ideas visually in ways I never thought possible. It's this personal evolution and empowerment that I hope to share with you throughout this book.

How To Use This Book

This guide is designed to be both sequential and flexible. Here's how to get the most out of your reading experience:

1. **Sequential Learning:**
   Start with the initial chapters to build a strong foundation in Canva's interface and basic design principles. Each chapter builds upon the previous one, ensuring a smooth learning curve.

2. **Interactive Exercises:**
   Throughout the book, you'll find practical exercises and mini-projects. Set aside time to work through these hands-on activities—they're integral to reinforcing your new skills. Don't be afraid to experiment; creativity thrives in practice.

3. **Use the Resources:**
   At the end of each chapter, additional resources and links are provided. These include video tutorials, downloadable templates, and access to online communities where you can share your work and gain feedback.

4. **Jump Around as Needed:**
   If you're already familiar with certain topics, feel free to skip ahead to chapters that challenge you or introduce new techniques. The book is structured so that each section is a self-contained guide on a specific aspect of Canva.

5. **Keep a Creative Journal:**
   Document your projects, experiments, and even your creative challenges. Reflecting on your progress will not only reinforce what you learn but also inspire new ideas and approaches.

6. **Join the Community:**
   Beyond these pages, Canva's global community is a vibrant space for collaboration and inspiration. Engage with fellow readers and designers through forums, social media groups, and workshops mentioned in the resource directory.

By following these suggestions, you'll be well-equipped to transform your ideas into compelling visual stories. The journey through this book is not just about acquiring technical skills—it's about igniting a passion for creativity that will continue to evolve long after you've turned the final page.

Embrace the adventure, experiment boldly, and remember: every great design starts with a single, inspired idea. Let's begin this journey together, one creative step at a time.

Introduction To Canva

Canva's emergence marks a turning point in the history of design—a revolution that has made creativity accessible to everyone. In this chapter, we'll explore the evolution of design tools, uncover what makes Canva so unique, and set the stage for cultivating a creative mindset.

The Evolution Of Design

Before Canva, design was often synonymous with complex software like Adobe Photoshop and Illustrator—tools that demanded a steep learning curve and significant time investment.

For decades, graphic design was largely the domain of professionals trained in intricate techniques and workflows. Traditional design software, while powerful, could feel inaccessible to non-designers who needed to communicate visually but lacked technical expertise.

Then came Canva. Launched in 2013, Canva introduced a simple, drag-and-drop interface paired with an extensive library of templates, photos, icons, and fonts. This innovation marked a pivotal shift in the design landscape. Canva didn't just add another tool to the market; it fundamentally democratized design by removing technical barriers. Suddenly, anyone with an idea could create professional-quality visuals without years of training. This approach not only empowered individuals and small businesses but also set off a wave of creativity across industries worldwide.

What Is Canva?

At its core, Canva is a web-based graphic design platform that offers a user-friendly alternative to traditional design software. It operates on a freemium model—providing essential tools for free, with the option to upgrade to Pro for advanced features. Whether you're a student, entrepreneur, educator, or hobbyist, Canva is built to meet your creative needs.

Key Features:

- **Intuitive Interface:**
  The drag-and-drop design editor makes it easy to assemble images, text, and elements without prior experience. Users can start with thousands of pre-designed templates tailored for social media posts, presentations, marketing materials, and more.

- **Freemium vs. Pro:**
  The free version of Canva provides ample functionality for most casual users, while

the Pro subscription unlocks premium assets, advanced editing features, and specialized tools like Magic Studio—a suite of AI-powered functionalities that streamline and enhance the design process. This tiered structure ensures that Canva remains accessible to everyone while offering power users the tools they need for professional projects.

- **Global Impact:**
Canva's ease of use and versatility have led to widespread adoption across the globe. With millions of users in over 190 countries, Canva has become a cultural phenomenon, leveling the playing field in visual communication. From individual creators to multinational corporations, its impact resonates far beyond traditional design boundaries.

Setting Your Creative Mindset

Embracing creativity starts with the right mindset. Whether you consider yourself an artist or someone who simply needs to communicate ideas visually, understanding design fundamentals and cultivating a creative approach are key.

Tips for Embracing Creativity:

- **Adopt a Growth Mindset:**
  Creativity is not a fixed trait—it's a skill that can be developed through practice and experimentation. Allow yourself the freedom to experiment without the fear of making mistakes. Every design, even those that don't turn out as expected, is a step forward in your creative journey.

- **Learn Design Fundamentals:**
  Start with the basics: understand color theory, typography, layout, and composition. Even a rudimentary grasp of these principles can dramatically elevate

the quality of your designs. Use Canva's extensive resources and tutorials as stepping stones to deepen your knowledge.

- **Seek Inspiration and Build a Visual Library:**
  Surround yourself with creative stimuli. Whether it's through online galleries, design blogs, or social media, constantly expose yourself to diverse aesthetics and ideas. Use Canva's built-in tools to create mood boards that compile your favorite designs and color palettes, which can serve as reference points for your own projects.

- **Embrace Iterative Design:**
  Good design is rarely perfect on the first try. Utilize Canva's easy editing tools to iterate on your ideas. Tweak layouts, adjust colors, and experiment with different fonts until your vision aligns

with your creative intent.

- **Connect with a Community:**
  One of Canva's most valuable assets is its community. Engage with fellow designers through forums, social media groups, and shared projects. Feedback and collaboration can provide fresh perspectives, sparking new ideas and helping you refine your style.

By setting a creative mindset and being open to continuous learning, you'll be well-prepared to harness the full potential of Canva. This foundation not only equips you to navigate the platform with ease but also encourages a broader, more innovative approach to visual communication.

In this chapter, we've traced the evolution of design from its traditional roots to the innovative, inclusive landscape enabled by Canva. We've seen how Canva's unique approach breaks down barriers and empowers users worldwide, and we've explored ways to foster a mindset that welcomes creativity. As you move forward in this book, keep these insights in mind—they form the backbone of your journey into the world of digital design.

Getting Started With Canva

This chapter serves as your first hands-on experience with Canva. We'll walk through creating your account, familiarizing yourself with the interface, and exploring how Canva adapts to different devices. Whether you're using a desktop, tablet, or smartphone, this chapter will ensure you have a solid foundation to launch your creative journey.

Creating Your Account

Step-by-Step Guide to Signing Up

1. **Visit the Canva Website or Download the App:**
   Start by navigating to Canva.com on your desktop browser, or download the Canva app from your device's app store. The website and app share a similar interface, ensuring a seamless experience regardless of your device.

2. **Sign Up Process:**

   ○ **Choose Your Sign-Up Option:** You can sign up using your email address, Google account, or Facebook. The process is streamlined, and using a social login can often speed up the registration process.

- ○ **Enter Your Details:** Provide your name, email, and create a password. Canva may also ask for additional information, such as your interests or intended use (personal, business, education), to tailor the experience.
- ○ **Email Verification:** After submitting your details, check your email for a verification link. Clicking this link will activate your account.

3. **Setting Up Your Profile:**

- ○ **Profile Customization:** Once your account is active, navigate to your account settings to add a profile picture, update your name, and optionally include a short bio. This not only personalizes your dashboard but also makes it easier to collaborate if you're working with a team.
- ○ **Choosing a Plan:** Canva operates on a freemium model. You can start

with the free version, which offers a robust set of features. For advanced tools—like premium templates, additional storage, and exclusive AI-powered functionalities—you may opt for Canva Pro or other professional tiers.

4. **Navigating the Dashboard:**
   After setting up your profile, you'll land on the Canva dashboard. Here, you'll find an organized layout of your projects, recent designs, and quick access to the template library. The dashboard is designed to be intuitive, letting you quickly jump into creating or editing designs.

Understanding the Interface

A thorough understanding of the Canva interface is crucial to maximizing your design potential. Let's explore the key areas of the interface:

Top Menu

- **Home:**
  This button brings you back to the main dashboard where you can view recent projects, access tutorials, and see featured templates.
- **Templates:**
  Browse thousands of pre-designed templates sorted by categories such as social media, presentations, posters, and more.
- **Features and Tools:**
  Quick access to elements like photos, illustrations, icons, charts, and text styles. These features are neatly categorized for ease of use.
- **Learn:**
  Access tutorials, design tips, and

inspiration. This section is particularly useful for beginners and those looking to expand their creative skills.

- **Pricing:**
  Information about Canva's freemium and Pro plans, detailing what additional features you can unlock by upgrading.

Side Panel

- **Your Projects:**
  Easily locate and organize your existing designs. You can create folders and tag projects to keep your work tidy.
- **Uploads:**
  A dedicated area where you can upload your own images, logos, and other media files. This helps you integrate personal assets into your designs.
- **Elements and Text:**
  Direct access to Canva's vast library of design elements such as shapes, icons, and customizable text boxes. The drag-and-drop functionality makes it

simple to add these elements to your canvas.

- **Additional Tools:**
  Features like the background remover, color palette generator, and animation tools are accessible from this panel, providing advanced customization options.

Key Features and Functionalities

- **Drag-and-Drop Editor:**
  Canva's intuitive editor allows you to place, resize, and rearrange elements effortlessly. This makes it ideal for both beginners and experienced designers.
- **Real-Time Editing:**
  Changes are saved automatically as you work, so you never have to worry about losing your progress.
- **Collaboration Tools:**
  Canva makes it easy to invite team members to edit or comment on your designs, fostering a collaborative creative environment.

Together, these features create an interface that is not only powerful but also inviting for users at all levels.

Device and Platform Flexibility

Canva's design is inherently versatile, catering to a wide range of devices and usage scenarios.

Desktop

- **Full-Featured Experience:**
  On desktops, Canva's interface is optimized for larger screens. The full suite of tools and panels is readily accessible, making it ideal for in-depth projects such as detailed presentations, marketing materials, or complex design layouts.
- **Browser Compatibility:**
  Canva works across major browsers like Chrome, Firefox, Safari, and Edge, ensuring that you can start designing without needing to install additional software.

Tablets

- **Touch-Friendly Interface:**
  Tablets offer a middle ground between the portability of smartphones and the functionality of desktops. Canva's interface adapts to touch controls, allowing for smooth drag-and-drop interactions and easy resizing of elements.
- **Portable Creativity:**
  With a tablet, you can create or edit designs on the go—ideal for brainstorming sessions, quick edits, or collaborating during meetings.

Smartphones

- **Optimized Mobile App:**
  Canva's mobile app provides a streamlined version of the desktop interface. It is optimized for smaller screens, making it easy to create social media posts, simple graphics, and quick edits.

- **Accessibility and Convenience:**
  The mobile app is designed for spontaneity. Whether you're capturing inspiration on the go or need to make a last-minute tweak before posting on social media, the app ensures you have powerful design tools at your fingertips.

Consistent Experience Across Platforms

- **Cloud Syncing:**
  Canva's cloud-based system means your projects are saved and accessible across all devices. Start a design on your desktop and finish it on your smartphone without missing a beat.
- **Unified User Interface:**
  Despite the differences in screen size, Canva maintains a consistent design and user experience across platforms, ensuring that the learning curve remains minimal regardless of the device you're using.

By understanding how to set up your account, navigate the interface, and utilize Canva on different devices, you're well-equipped to dive into the creative process. This chapter lays the groundwork for a smooth, enjoyable design journey—one that empowers you to create stunning visuals wherever you are.

Embrace the flexibility and power of Canva as you begin exploring your creative potential. Whether you're at home, in the office, or on the move, Canva's platform is designed to meet you where you are and support your vision every step of the way.

Design Fundamentals and Principles

Design is both an art and a science. In this chapter, we explore the core principles that underpin every great visual creation—from color theory and typography to composition and balance. By understanding these basics, you'll be able to transform your ideas into compelling, aesthetically pleasing designs using Canva.

Basic Design Theory

Color Theory

Color is the heartbeat of visual communication. A well-chosen palette can evoke emotion, create emphasis, and even guide the viewer's eye. Key concepts include:

- **Color Wheel:** Understand primary, secondary, and tertiary colors and how they interact.
- **Harmony and Contrast:** Learn about complementary, analogous, and triadic color schemes to create balance or vibrant contrasts.
- **Psychological Impact:** Different colors trigger different emotions—for example, blue often conveys trust and calm, while red can evoke passion or urgency.

Typography

Typography goes beyond just picking a font—it sets the tone for your entire design.

- **Font Pairing:** Learn how to combine fonts (such as serif with sans-serif) for readability and visual appeal.
- **Hierarchy:** Establish a clear hierarchy with headings, subheadings, and body text to guide the viewer through your message.
- **Spacing and Alignment:** Effective use of line spacing (leading), letter spacing (tracking), and proper alignment can make a world of difference in legibility and design aesthetics.

Composition and Layout

The way elements are arranged in your design determines its overall impact.

- **Rule of Thirds:** Divide your canvas into a 3x3 grid to place key elements at intersecting points, creating a balanced composition.
- **Visual Flow:** Guide the viewer's eye through the design using strategic placements of images, text, and white space.

- **Balance and Symmetry:** Achieve a harmonious design by balancing elements either symmetrically or asymmetrically.

Balance

Balance is about creating a sense of stability in your design.

- **Symmetrical Balance:** Mirrored elements on either side of a central axis create a formal and orderly design.
- **Asymmetrical Balance:** Different visual weights (color, size, shape) are arranged to create a dynamic yet balanced composition.

Inspiration and Mood Boards

Gathering Inspiration

Great design often starts with great inspiration. Here are ways to fuel your creativity:

- **Online Galleries and Portfolios:** Explore design communities like Behance or Pinterest to see trending styles and unique ideas.
- **Industry Trends:** Follow design blogs and Canva's own inspiration pages to keep up with emerging trends.
- **Nature and Everyday Life:** Sometimes the best ideas come from the world around you—textures, colors, and patterns in your environment can spark creativity.

Creating Mood Boards in Canva

Mood boards are an essential tool for consolidating inspiration and setting the visual tone for your projects.

- **Collecting Visual Elements:** Use Canva to compile images, color swatches, fonts, and other design elements that resonate with your vision.
- **Digital Collage:** Drag and drop your selected assets onto a blank canvas,

arrange them creatively, and annotate with notes or keywords.

- **Iterative Process:** Update your mood board as your ideas evolve. This living document helps you stay focused on your design goals and provides a reference point for consistency.

Practical Exercises

To solidify your understanding of design fundamentals, try these hands-on projects:

Exercise 1: Create a Color Palette

- **Task:** Choose a theme (e.g., "Serenity" or "Energy") and create a color palette using Canva's color tools. Experiment with complementary and analogous schemes.
- **Goal:** Understand how different color combinations evoke varying emotions and set the tone for your design.

Exercise 2: Typography Pairing Challenge

- **Task:** Create a simple poster using two contrasting fonts. Play with hierarchy—use one font for the headline and another for the body text.
- **Goal:** Learn how font choices and pairings can enhance readability and visual impact.

Exercise 3: Layout and Composition

- **Task:** Design a social media graphic using the rule of thirds and balanced layout principles. Arrange images, text, and icons in a way that guides the viewer's eye naturally.
- **Goal:** Practice creating a harmonious layout that balances visual elements effectively.

Exercise 4: Build a Mood Board

- **Task:** Start a new project in Canva and create a mood board for an upcoming project. Gather images, color swatches, and inspirational quotes, then arrange them in a collage format.

- **Goal:** Develop a visual reference that will guide your design projects and help maintain a cohesive aesthetic.

By exploring these fundamental principles and engaging in practical exercises, you'll begin to see design not as a daunting discipline but as a series of interconnected concepts that can be mastered with practice. Whether you're refining an existing project or embarking on a new creative venture, understanding and applying these design fundamentals will be the cornerstone of your success in Canva.

Embrace these principles as you build your creative toolkit. Remember, every expert was once a beginner, and every design is an opportunity to learn, iterate, and ultimately shine.

Navigating Canva's Templates and Tools

One of Canva's greatest strengths is its powerful, yet user-friendly set of templates and tools that empower you to create stunning designs without the steep learning curve of traditional graphic design software. In this chapter, we'll delve into the rich template library, explore customization essentials, and master the drag-and-drop interface that makes design both intuitive and efficient.

Template Library Overview

Canva offers an extensive library of templates designed for virtually every need, whether you're creating a social media post, an engaging presentation, a compelling marketing flyer, or even a detailed infographic. Here's how to make the most of this resource:

- **Diverse Categories:**
  From Instagram stories and Facebook posts to resumes, business cards, newsletters, and more, Canva's template library is organized by category. This ensures you can quickly find a design that fits your project's purpose.

- **Industry-Specific Designs:**
  Whether you're in education, business, or creative arts, you'll find templates tailored to your niche. The designs incorporate current trends and best practices, ensuring your visuals are both modern and professional.

- **High-Quality, Professionally Designed Assets:**
  Each template is crafted by experienced designers and can serve as a strong starting point for your work. These templates are fully customizable, allowing you to adapt them to your brand's unique look and feel.

- **Regular Updates:**
  Canva frequently adds new templates and updates its library to reflect the latest design trends, so you're always equipped with fresh ideas to inspire your projects.

- **Search and Filter Tools:**
  With powerful search and filter options, you can quickly narrow down templates by style, format, or purpose, making the process of finding the perfect starting point both quick and enjoyable.

Customization Essentials

While the pre-designed templates offer a great foundation, the true power of Canva lies in its flexibility. Customization lets you infuse your personality and brand identity into every project. Here's how to fine-tune your chosen template:

- **Modifying Text and Typography:** Change text elements with ease—edit headlines, subheadings, and body text by simply clicking on the text boxes. Canva allows you to select from a vast range of fonts, adjust font sizes, line spacing, and letter spacing, and even pair different font styles to create a clear hierarchy that directs your audience's attention.

- **Adjusting Colors and Themes:** Canva provides intuitive color editing tools that enable you to align a design with your brand's color palette. Whether you want to change the background color or adjust individual elements, you can apply custom colors or select from preset palettes.

- **Resizing and Rearranging Layouts:**
  The drag-and-drop functionality means you can easily move elements around, resize images, or adjust the spacing between objects. This flexibility allows you to experiment with layout variations until you find the perfect balance.

- **Incorporating Images and Icons:**
  Replace placeholder images with your own photos or choose from Canva's extensive library of high-quality stock images and icons. You can also adjust image filters, crop photos, or use advanced features like the background remover to integrate your visuals seamlessly.

- **Layering and Effects:**
  Customize the depth and interaction of elements using layering options. Bring attention to key elements with effects such

as drop shadows, transparency adjustments, or blurring, ensuring that your design communicates the intended message effectively.

- **Saving and Reusing Customized Templates:**
  Once you've tailored a template to meet your needs, save it as a custom template for future projects. This not only streamlines your workflow but also helps maintain consistency across your designs.

Utilizing Drag-and-Drop

At the heart of Canva's ease-of-use is its powerful drag-and-drop interface. This intuitive feature transforms the design process into a tactile and interactive experience:

- **Seamless Movement:**
  Simply click on any element—be it text,

an image, or an icon—and drag it to your desired location on the canvas. The interface highlights drop zones and offers guides, making alignment a breeze.

- **Instant Customization:**
  As you drag elements, Canva allows you to resize, rotate, and adjust them on the fly. This real-time editing capability means you can experiment with different arrangements without interrupting your creative flow.

- **Smart Guides and Grid Lines:**
  Canva's built-in alignment guides help you maintain a professional layout. These smart guides ensure that your elements are evenly spaced and aligned, taking the guesswork out of composition.

- **Effortless Layering:**
  Manage overlapping elements easily with layering controls. You can bring an element forward or send it back to create

depth, ensuring that every part of your design contributes to the overall aesthetic.

- **Intuitive Interactions:**
  The simplicity of dragging and dropping extends to adding new elements from the side panel, rearranging sections of your design, or even integrating text and graphics together. This makes Canva a favorite among both beginners and experienced designers who value speed and flexibility.

- **Responsive Design Across Devices:**
  Whether you're working on a desktop, tablet, or smartphone, the drag-and-drop interface remains consistent, ensuring that your design experience is smooth and efficient no matter where you create.

Putting It All Together

By exploring the template library, mastering customization, and leveraging the drag-and-drop interface, you unlock Canva's full potential. This chapter empowers you to:

- Start with professionally designed templates that spark your creativity.
- Modify every element to ensure your design is unique and aligned with your vision.
- Use the intuitive drag-and-drop system to create visually appealing and well-organized designs quickly.

As you work through your projects, remember that each template is a starting point—a canvas waiting for your creative touch. Experiment, iterate, and don't hesitate to explore new layouts or combinations of elements. With Canva's tools at your disposal, the possibilities for creative expression are virtually limitless.

Embrace this journey of design exploration, and let each project be a testament to your evolving creative expertise.

Working With Visual Elements

Visual elements are the heartbeat of any design. In this chapter, we'll dive into how you can work effectively with various visual assets in Canva—from finding and editing images to harnessing the power of text, icons, shapes, and even your own media uploads. Mastering these elements will empower you to create designs that communicate clearly, engage your audience, and elevate your brand.

Images and Illustrations

Images and illustrations provide the visual narrative in your designs. Canva's extensive library gives you access to millions of stock photos, illustrations, and graphics, ensuring that you have the right visual for every project.

Finding the Perfect Visuals

- **Stock Photos and Graphics:**
  Canva's library includes over two million free and premium stock images available for personal and commercial use. Whether you need a high-resolution photo for a blog post or an eye-catching illustration for a marketing flyer, you can easily search by theme, category, or even by color to find visuals that match your aesthetic.

- **Diverse Styles:**
  From modern minimalistic designs to vibrant, dynamic illustrations, Canva's resource pool caters to all tastes and

industries. This diversity allows you to explore various styles until you discover the perfect match for your project.

Editing and Enhancing Images

- **Built-in Photo Editor:**
  Once you've chosen an image, Canva's free online photo editor lets you crop, adjust brightness, contrast, and saturation, and even apply filters to create a consistent look across your designs. You can also remove backgrounds or add overlays to enhance the visual appeal.

- **Creative Adjustments:**
  Use Canva's editing tools to add text overlays, blend modes, and artistic effects that help your images align with your brand's visual language. These modifications not only improve the aesthetics but also reinforce your message.

Incorporating Illustrations

- **Vector Illustrations and Icons:**
  In addition to photos, Canva offers a vast range of illustrations and vector graphics that can be resized without losing quality. This flexibility is particularly useful for creating logos, infographics, and other scalable assets.

- **Customization:**
  Many illustrations can be recolored, reshaped, or layered with other elements, giving you the freedom to adjust them to fit your specific design requirements.

Text and Typography

Text isn't just about conveying information—it also plays a crucial role in establishing the tone, hierarchy, and overall look of your design.

Adding and Editing Text

- **Text Boxes and Presets:**
  Canva makes it easy to add text through its intuitive text boxes. You can choose from preset text styles, which include a variety of combinations of font styles, sizes, and spacing tailored for different purposes (headlines, body text, captions, etc.).

- **Formatting Tools:**
  With the text editing toolbar, you can modify font size, style, color, spacing, and alignment. This granular control ensures that your text not only looks good but also supports the design's overall visual balance.

Choosing the Right Fonts

- **Font Pairing:**
  Effective typography is all about balance. Use contrasting fonts (like pairing a serif

headline with a sans-serif body) to create visual interest and clarity. Canva provides recommendations and pairings that work well together, making it easier for you to experiment without compromising on style.

- **Brand Consistency:**
  Incorporate your brand's signature fonts by uploading custom fonts (a feature available with Canva Pro) and saving them in your Brand Kit. This ensures consistency across all your projects and helps reinforce brand identity.

Advanced Text Effects

- **Creative Enhancements:**
  Use Canva's text effects to add shadows, outlines, or even animated text. These effects can give your typography a unique flair that makes your message stand out.

- **Text-to-Shape Integration:**
  For added creativity, experiment with placing text within shapes or along paths. While this might require a bit more manual adjustment, it can transform a simple design into something truly dynamic.

Icons, Shapes, and Elements

Icons, shapes, and other design elements can elevate a layout by adding visual cues, breaking up text, and guiding the viewer's eye through the content.

Utilizing Canva's Library

- **Vast Collection:**
  Canva offers a rich library of icons, shapes, lines, and other graphic elements that can be easily integrated into your designs. Whether you need an arrow to

guide viewers or a decorative border, the options are plentiful.

- **Search and Filter:**
  Use keywords to search for specific icons or shapes that align with your project's theme. You can filter by style (flat, outline, 3D, etc.) to maintain a cohesive look.

Customizing Elements

- **Color and Size Adjustments:**
  Once added to your design, icons and shapes can be resized, recolored, and repositioned. This customization ensures that they harmonize with your overall color scheme and layout.

- **Layering and Grouping:**
  Arrange elements in layers to create depth and dimension in your design. Canva's grouping feature allows you to combine multiple elements so that they

move and resize as one unit.

Enhancing Your Design

- **Visual Hierarchy:**
  Use icons and shapes to create a visual hierarchy. For example, a bold icon can draw attention to a key point, while subtle shapes can frame content or separate sections.

- **Interactive Design:**
  Consider using animated icons or dynamic shapes to add movement to digital projects. Animation options can help engage viewers, particularly in social media or web designs.

Uploading Your Own Media

Sometimes, stock resources just won't capture your unique vision. Canva allows you to upload your own images, logos, and videos to create fully customized designs.

Steps to Import Custom Media

- **Access the Uploads Panel:**
  On the left side of the Canva interface, click the "Uploads" tab. Here, you'll see an option to "Upload Media." Click this button to open your device's file browser.

- **Supported File Formats:**
  Canva supports a range of file formats including JPEG, PNG, SVG (for vectors), and MP4 for videos. Ensure your files are in one of these formats to guarantee compatibility.

- **Drag-and-Drop Functionality:**
  You can also drag files directly from your computer into the Uploads panel. This

feature makes it easy to quickly add multiple files at once.

Organizing and Using Uploaded Media

- **Creating Folders:**
  To keep your media organized, Canva allows you to create folders within the Uploads section. This is particularly useful if you work on multiple projects or need to store a variety of brand assets.

- **Editing Custom Media:**
  Once uploaded, you can click on your media to add it to your design. Use Canva's built-in editing tools to crop, apply filters, or adjust image settings. This ensures that your custom visuals match the look and feel of the rest of your design.

- **Integrating with Other Elements:**
  Custom media can be layered with stock images, text, and other elements to create

a cohesive design. For instance, you might upload your logo and position it alongside stock photos and icons to create branded marketing materials.

By mastering these visual elements—whether leveraging Canva's extensive library or importing your own assets—you'll be able to create designs that are both visually stunning and uniquely yours. Experiment, iterate, and let your creativity flow as you blend images, text, icons, and custom media into cohesive and impactful visuals.

Each section in this chapter is designed to build your confidence and skills, ensuring that every visual element you use enhances the overall message and aesthetic of your work. Happy designing!

Advanced Design Techniques with Canva

As you become more comfortable with Canva's fundamental features, it's time to explore advanced techniques that will elevate your designs to a professional level. In this chapter, we dive deep into AI-powered enhancements, dynamic animations, intricate layering, and efficient export and file management practices. These advanced methods not only streamline your workflow but also open up a world of creative possibilities.

Magic Studio and AI Tools

Canva's Magic Studio is a game changer, integrating a suite of AI-powered features that simplify complex design tasks and spark innovation.

Magic Design and Magic Edit

- **Magic Design:**
  This feature transforms your design brief into fully realized layouts in seconds. Simply input a text prompt or upload an inspiring image, and Magic Design generates several layout options that you can customize further. This tool is perfect for brainstorming ideas quickly or kickstarting projects when you're short on time.

- **Magic Edit:**
  Gone are the days of laborious manual adjustments. With Magic Edit, you can

brush over any element in your image—such as changing colors or removing distractions—and simply describe your desired change in words. Powered by advanced AI algorithms, Magic Edit makes subtle tweaks that enhance the overall look of your design without compromising its integrity.

Other AI-Powered Features

- **Magic Eraser and Magic Grab:** Need to remove an unwanted object from a photo or reposition a subject? Magic Eraser quickly removes distractions, while Magic Grab isolates and repositions the main subject seamlessly, ensuring a polished result.

- **Magic Expand and Magic Animate:** Magic Expand intelligently enlarges image borders to fix composition issues, and Magic Animate provides a suite of animation options that can breathe life into static designs by adding smooth transitions and dynamic effects.

These AI tools not only save time but also empower you to experiment with ideas you might not have attempted manually. They continuously evolve, integrating improvements that keep your designs fresh and innovative.

Animation and Interactivity

Dynamic, animated content captures attention and engages viewers more effectively than static images.

Creating Animated Presentations and Social Media Posts

- **Animation Options:**
  Canva's Magic Animate allows you to apply various animation styles—such as "Pop," "Drift," or "Tectonic"—to individual elements within your design.

These animations are perfect for presentations, social media posts, or even website graphics, where a subtle movement can make your design stand out.

- **Interactive Elements:**
  Beyond simple animations, Canva supports interactive features like clickable buttons, transitions, and even interactive charts. These tools enable you to create engaging multimedia presentations that can respond to user interactions, making your content more immersive.

Interactive Charts and Data Visualizations

- **Dynamic Data Presentation:**
  Use Canva's interactive chart tools to transform static data into visually compelling graphs and infographics. With customizable animation and transition effects, your charts can guide viewers through the data narrative smoothly and

clearly.

- **Real-Time Collaboration:**
  In collaborative projects, interactive
  whiteboards and live reaction stickers
  foster teamwork and real-time idea
  exchange, ensuring that your design
  process is as dynamic as your final
  product.

These animation and interactivity features not
only enhance viewer engagement but also add a
modern, professional polish to your digital
designs.

Layering and Grouping Techniques

Advanced management of design elements is
crucial for creating sophisticated and balanced
layouts.

Mastering Layers

- **Z-Index Control:**
  Understanding how to arrange elements in layers is fundamental. Canva's layering tools let you bring elements forward or send them backward, enabling you to create depth and hierarchy in your design. This is particularly useful when working with complex images or overlapping elements.

- **Using Transparency and Effects:**
  Adjusting transparency levels on different layers can create subtle visual effects and emphasize focal points. Coupling transparency with shadow and blur effects can make your design appear more three-dimensional and refined.

Grouping Elements for Consistency

- **Efficient Grouping:**
  Group similar elements together to maintain alignment and consistency. This is especially useful when you need to

move, resize, or apply effects to multiple items at once. Grouping streamlines your workflow and ensures that related components stay perfectly aligned.

- **Dynamic Adjustments:**
  With advanced grouping techniques, you can create templates that allow for dynamic changes. For instance, by grouping text with background shapes, you can update your content while preserving the overall layout integrity.

Employing these layering and grouping strategies helps you manage complex designs with ease, resulting in a cohesive and professional final product.

Exporting and File Management

Once your design is perfected, proper exporting and organization are key to maintaining efficiency and ensuring your work is ready for use across various platforms.

Best Practices for Exporting Designs

- **Choosing the Right Format:**
  Canva offers multiple export formats, including PNG, JPEG, PDF, and MP4 for animated projects. Select the format that best suits your intended use—for example, PNG for high-quality images with transparency, JPEG for web images, and PDF for print materials.

- **Optimizing Resolution and Quality:**
  Always check your export settings to ensure the resolution is appropriate for your project. For social media, a resolution of 1080 x 1080 pixels is often ideal, while print projects may require

higher resolutions.

Organizing Your Projects

- **Creating a File Naming System:**
  Develop a consistent naming convention for your files and folders. This practice helps in quickly locating projects and maintaining version control, especially when collaborating with a team.

- **Cloud Storage and Backup:**
  Canva's cloud-based platform automatically saves your work, but it's good practice to periodically export and backup your files locally or on a secondary cloud storage service. This ensures you never lose your progress and can access previous versions when needed.

- **Template Management:**
  Save frequently used designs as custom templates in Canva. This not only saves

time for future projects but also ensures brand consistency across multiple designs.

By following these export and file management best practices, you'll ensure that your advanced designs are not only visually stunning but also optimized for their intended medium and easy to manage over time.

Embracing these advanced design techniques in Canva transforms your creative process from basic design to professional artistry. By harnessing AI-powered Magic Studio tools, animating your content for interactivity, mastering intricate layering, and managing your exports efficiently, you open the door to limitless creative possibilities. Happy designing!

Collaborative Design and Team Projects

Working in a collaborative environment can transform the creative process, ensuring that diverse ideas and perspectives come together to produce polished, consistent, and innovative designs. In this chapter, we explore advanced strategies for setting up teams, sharing work and feedback, and organizing projects within Canva, so that teams—whether small or large—can work seamlessly together.

Creating and Managing Teams

Setting Up Your Team in Canva

- **Canva Teams Overview:**
  Canva's collaborative tools enable you to create a dedicated team space where members can work on designs simultaneously. Once you sign in, navigate to the "Create a team" option on your dashboard. Here, you can invite colleagues via email and assign roles (such as editor or viewer) based on the level of access they require.

- **Inviting Members and Defining Roles:**
  Use the built-in invitation feature to add team members, ensuring they receive an email with a direct link to join your team workspace. Roles can be customized to control editing permissions and access to brand assets, such as logos, colors, and fonts. This ensures that every member contributes within defined boundaries to

maintain brand consistency.

- **Integrating the Brand Kit:**
  For businesses and organizations, setting up a Brand Kit within your team is essential. This centralized hub stores your brand's colors, fonts, logos, and templates, allowing every team member to access and utilize consistent design elements across all projects.

Best Practices for Team Collaboration

- **Clear Communication Channels:**
  Establish regular check-ins and designate specific channels (within Canva's commenting system or via external tools) to discuss design changes and creative direction. This helps avoid confusion and keeps everyone aligned with the project goals.

- **Defining Workflow Processes:**
  Outline clear steps for design review,

approval, and iteration. This might include assigning a team leader to provide final sign-off or using Canva's version history feature to track revisions and changes.

- **Utilizing Shared Folders:**
  Create dedicated folders for each project or campaign. Shared folders make it easier for team members to locate and update files and ensure that everyone is working on the latest version of a design.

Sharing and Feedback

Leveraging Canva's Sharing Options

- **Instant Sharing:**
  Canva allows you to share designs directly via a link. You can set the permissions to allow others to view, comment on, or edit the design, making it easy to circulate drafts among

stakeholders.

- **Commenting Features:**
  In collaborative projects, the commenting feature is invaluable. Team members can leave feedback directly on specific elements of a design. Comments are timestamped and tagged with the author's name, ensuring that all feedback is organized and easy to follow.

- **Version Control and History:**
  Canva's version control system automatically saves your progress. If you need to revert to an earlier version or compare changes over time, the version history feature lets you do so, ensuring that no creative idea is lost and making it easier to track collaborative contributions.

Gathering and Incorporating Feedback

- **Real-Time Collaboration:**
  With real-time editing, team members can

see each other's changes as they happen. This immediate visual feedback is crucial during brainstorming sessions or when working under tight deadlines.

- **Interactive Reviews:**
  Encourage team members to use Canva's live review sessions. During these sessions, designers can present their work to the team, gather immediate feedback, and discuss potential improvements—all within the platform.

- **Integrating External Feedback:**
  If your team uses external tools like Slack or Trello for project management, integrate Canva's share links and screenshots into these systems to centralize feedback and keep all stakeholders in the loop.

Project Organization

Creating a Consistent Design System

- **Organizing Projects with Folders:**
  Use Canva's folder system to categorize projects by client, campaign, or department. This helps maintain order and makes it easy for team members to find past work, templates, and assets.

- **Naming Conventions and Tagging:**
  Establish a clear naming convention for files and projects. Consistent file names and tags not only speed up searchability but also ensure that team members can quickly understand the project's context without having to open each file.

- **Template Libraries:**
  Save frequently used designs as custom templates. This allows your team to maintain a consistent look and feel across different projects and reduces the time

spent recreating basic layouts.

Efficient File Management

- **Cloud-Based Storage:**
  Since Canva is cloud-based, your projects
  are automatically saved and synced.
  However, it's still a good practice to
  periodically export final versions of
  designs for backup or offline access.

- **Versioning and Documentation:**
  Keep a log of major revisions and
  decisions made during the design process.
  Documenting changes not only helps in
  maintaining a record of your creative
  evolution but also assists in onboarding
  new team members.

- **Access Control:**
  Set permissions for who can view, edit, or
  delete projects. This minimizes the risk of
  accidental alterations and ensures that
  only authorized team members can make

significant changes.

By harnessing these collaborative tools and organizational strategies, teams can work more efficiently and creatively. Canva's robust features for team management, sharing and feedback, and project organization make it easier than ever to bring diverse ideas together, resulting in polished designs that resonate with your audience. Embrace these techniques to foster a culture of collaboration and innovation, and watch as your collective creative vision comes to life.

Canva for Business and Marketing

In today's fast-paced digital landscape, a strong visual presence is essential for any business. Canva not only empowers individuals but also transforms the way companies build their brand, market their products, and communicate their message. This chapter explores how Canva can be leveraged for business and marketing through robust branding, engaging social media content, persuasive presentations, and inspiring success stories.

Branding Essentials

Building a Consistent Brand Identity

Creating a memorable brand starts with visual consistency. Canva's Brand Kit is designed to help businesses establish and maintain a cohesive identity. With the Brand Kit, you can:

- **Store and Organize Assets:**
  Upload your logos, choose your brand colors, and select your signature fonts so that every design adheres to your established visual identity.
- **Custom Templates:**
  Save your favorite layouts as custom templates to ensure that every marketing material, whether an email header, social media post, or brochure, looks consistent.
- **Easy Updates:**
  As your brand evolves, updating your Brand Kit means that every design you

create automatically reflects your new identity.

This centralized control over your visual elements not only enhances recognition but also streamlines the creative process for teams, ensuring that every piece of communication is on-brand.

Leveraging Canva's Tools for Branding

Canva makes it simple to experiment with new ideas while maintaining brand consistency. Use features like:

- **Custom Font Uploads:**
  Integrate your unique typography into your designs (available with Canva Pro) to reinforce your brand's personality.
- **Color Palette Generator:**
  Match your designs to your brand colors effortlessly.
- **Pre-Designed Templates:**
  Choose from a variety of business and

marketing templates that can be tailored to your specific needs.

Social Media and Content Marketing

Optimizing Content for Social Platforms

Social media is a critical channel for brand engagement. Canva provides pre-set dimensions for various platforms, ensuring that your designs are optimized whether they're on Instagram, Facebook, LinkedIn, or Twitter. Here's how you can harness Canva for your content marketing efforts:

- **Tailored Designs:**
  Utilize platform-specific templates—such as Instagram Stories, Facebook posts, and LinkedIn banners—to create content that fits perfectly on each channel.
- **Engaging Visuals:**
  Incorporate animations, infographics, and

high-quality images to capture attention
and drive engagement.
- **Consistent Messaging:**
  By using your Brand Kit, every social
  media post reinforces your visual identity,
  making your brand instantly recognizable
  across all channels.

Designing Ads and Promotional Materials

Canva also simplifies the creation of paid
advertising materials. Use its intuitive interface
to:

- **Develop Eye-Catching Ads:**
  Design ads that pop with bold visuals,
  clear call-to-actions, and engaging copy.
- **A/B Testing:**
  Quickly generate variations of a design to
  test which visuals resonate best with your
  audience.
- **Streamline Campaigns:**
  Save and replicate successful designs
  across campaigns to maintain a consistent
  message and look.

Presentation and Proposal Design

Creating Persuasive Business Presentations

A well-crafted presentation can be the key to winning over clients and investors. Canva's presentation templates are designed to be both professional and visually appealing:

- **Dynamic Slides:**
  Incorporate animations, transitions, and multimedia elements to keep your audience engaged.
- **Data Visualization:**
  Use interactive charts, graphs, and infographics to clearly communicate data and insights.
- **Customizable Layouts:**
  Tailor your presentation templates to reflect your brand's aesthetic, ensuring that every slide supports your overall message.

Designing Marketing Materials and Proposals

Beyond presentations, Canva excels at creating a wide range of marketing collateral including proposals, flyers, brochures, and business cards. With its drag-and-drop interface, you can:

- **Focus on Key Messaging:**
  Highlight your value propositions using bold typography and striking visuals.
- **Streamline Revision Processes:**
  Easily update and iterate on designs based on client or stakeholder feedback using Canva's version control and commenting features.
- **Export in Multiple Formats:**
  Deliver your materials in formats optimized for both digital distribution and high-quality print.

Case Studies

Success Stories of Brands Leveraging Canva

Real-world examples illustrate how Canva has transformed business practices:

- **Small Business Breakthrough:**
  A boutique startup used Canva to design a full suite of marketing materials—from social media graphics to customer proposals—without hiring a full-time designer. By leveraging Canva's Brand Kit and custom templates, they maintained a consistent look across all channels, which boosted their brand recognition and increased sales by 35% within the first quarter.

- **Enterprise-Level Consistency:**
  A multinational corporation integrated Canva into their marketing workflow to streamline the creation of digital assets

across global teams. By using shared Brand Kits and collaborative folders, they ensured that every branch of the company adhered to the same branding guidelines, which helped them launch a successful global campaign that increased online engagement by over 50%.

- **Entrepreneurial Innovation:** An individual entrepreneur launched a new product line using Canva to create compelling social media ads, email newsletters, and a professional business proposal. The ease of use and rich library of templates allowed them to iterate quickly, leading to a 25% increase in customer inquiries and a rapid growth in market share.

These case studies demonstrate that whether you're a solo entrepreneur or part of a large organization, Canva offers the tools needed to elevate your business communications and marketing efforts.

By integrating these advanced business and marketing strategies into your workflow, Canva becomes much more than just a design tool—it becomes a comprehensive solution for brand building and market communication. Embrace these techniques to ensure your business materials are not only visually stunning but also consistently aligned with your brand's identity, driving growth and engagement in the competitive digital marketplace.

Canva in Education and Nonprofit Sectors

In an era where visual communication is paramount, both educational institutions and nonprofit organizations are continually seeking tools that enhance their outreach and engagement. Canva emerges as a versatile platform catering to these sectors, offering intuitive design capabilities that empower educators, students, and nonprofit professionals alike.

Empowering Educators

Utilizing Canva for Classroom Projects

Canva provides educators with a plethora of resources to enrich classroom experiences:

- **Lesson Planning and Materials:** Teachers can craft visually appealing lesson plans, worksheets, and handouts, making learning materials more engaging for students.

- **Interactive Whiteboards:** With Canva's whiteboard feature, educators can create interactive brainstorming sessions, allowing students to collaborate in real-time, fostering creativity and critical thinking.

Digital Storytelling in Education

Digital storytelling transforms traditional narratives into dynamic, interactive experiences that captivate students' imaginations. Canva simplifies this process:

- **Storyboarding Tools:**
  Students can design storyboards, organize their thoughts and visualize the flow of their narratives effectively.

- **Multimedia Integration:**
  Incorporating images, videos, and audio elements is seamless, enabling students to produce rich, multimedia stories that enhance their learning experience.

Access to Educational Resources

Canva offers a vast array of resources tailored for educational purposes:

- **Template Library:**
  Educators have access to thousands of customizable templates suitable for various subjects and educational levels, streamlining the creation of instructional

materials.

- **Professional Development:**
  Through webinars and workshops, such
  as the "Mastering Digital Storytelling with
  Canva for Education," teachers can
  enhance their skills and stay updated with
  innovative teaching strategies.

Student Projects and Collaboration

Engaging Students in Creative Projects

Canva fosters student engagement by providing
tools that make learning interactive and
enjoyable:

- **Design Assignments:**
  Students can create posters, infographics,
  and presentations, allowing them to
  express their understanding creatively.

- **Collaborative Projects:**
  Canva's platform supports group work,
  enabling multiple students to collaborate
  on a single project simultaneously,
  promoting teamwork and communication
  skills.

Enhancing Learning Through Visuals

Visual aids are crucial in reinforcing learning
concepts:

- **Infographic Creation:**
  Students can distill complex information
  into concise infographics, aiding in better
  comprehension and retention of subject
  matter.

- **Presentation Skills:**
  By designing their own slides, students
  not only learn the subject content but also
  develop essential skills in visual
  communication and public speaking.

Nonprofit Initiatives

Amplifying Messaging and Outreach

Nonprofit organizations often operate with limited resources, making cost-effective tools like Canva invaluable:

- **Brand Consistency:**
  With Canva's Brand Kit, nonprofits can maintain a cohesive visual identity across all materials, enhancing brand recognition and trust among their audience.

- **Social Media Engagement:**
  Canva offers templates optimized for various social media platforms, enabling nonprofits to create compelling posts that drive engagement and awareness for their causes.

Access to Premium Features

Recognizing the vital role of nonprofits, Canva extends premium services to these organizations:

- **Canva for Nonprofits Program:**
  Eligible nonprofits can access Canva Pro features at no cost, unlocking advanced design tools, a vast media library, and collaborative functionalities to enhance their outreach efforts.

- **Resource Hub:**
  The Canva Nonprofit Resource Page provides tutorials, case studies, and design inspiration, assisting organizations in maximizing the platform's potential to further their missions.

By integrating Canva into educational and nonprofit activities, users can harness the power of visual communication to inspire, educate, and effect change. Its user-friendly interface, coupled with a wealth of resources, makes it an indispensable tool for those striving to make a meaningful impact in their communities.

Monetizing Your Designs with Canva

In the digital age, the demand for compelling visual content has surged, creating lucrative opportunities for designers and creatives. Canva, with its user-friendly interface and extensive design tools, has become a cornerstone for individuals aiming to monetize their design skills. This chapter delves into various avenues for generating income through Canva, including freelancing, creating digital products, self-publishing, and building a professional portfolio.

Freelancing and Digital Products

Creating and Selling Digital Products

The market for digital products is expansive, encompassing items like ebooks, social media templates, printables, and more. Canva simplifies the creation process, enabling designers to produce high-quality digital assets without the need for advanced software.

Popular Digital Products:

- **Ebooks and Magazines:** Design informative and visually appealing ebooks or digital magazines on topics you are passionate about.

- **Social Media Templates:** Create customizable templates for platforms like Instagram, Facebook, and LinkedIn, assisting businesses and influencers in maintaining a cohesive online presence.

- **Printables:** Design planners, calendars, worksheets, and art prints that customers can download and print at their convenience.

Platforms for Selling Digital Products:

Once your products are ready, various online marketplaces can help you reach a broad audience:

- **Etsy:** A popular platform for selling unique, handcrafted, and digital items.

- **Creative Market:** A marketplace for design assets, including templates, fonts, and graphics.

- **Teachers Pay Teachers:** Ideal for educational materials and printables.

Licensing Considerations:

When using Canva's resources, it's crucial to adhere to their Content License Agreement. Both Free and Pro users can create products for sale, but designs must be original and not directly resell Canva's unaltered content. For instance, using Canva to design templates or printables for sale is permissible, but selling unmodified Canva elements as standalone products is not allowed.

Offering Freelance Design Services

Canva's versatility makes it an excellent tool for freelance designers. You can offer services such as creating marketing materials, branding assets, and social media graphics for clients. Utilizing Canva allows for efficient collaboration and quick turnaround times, enhancing client satisfaction.

Steps to Start Freelancing with Canva:

1. **Identify Your Niche:** Determine the specific design services you want to offer, such as social media management,

branding, or content creation.

2. **Build a Portfolio:** Use Canva to create a portfolio showcasing your best work, making it easier to attract potential clients.

3. **Set Competitive Pricing:** Research industry standards to price your services appropriately.

4. **Market Your Services:** Utilize social media platforms, freelance websites, and personal networks to promote your offerings.

Self-Publishing with Canva

The rise of self-publishing has empowered authors to take control of their work, from creation to distribution. Canva provides a comprehensive suite of tools to design professional-quality books without the need for extensive graphic design experience.

Designing Book Covers and Interiors

Book Covers:

A compelling cover is vital for attracting readers. Canva offers customizable templates tailored for various genres, allowing you to design eye-catching covers that align with your book's theme.

Interiors:

Formatting the interior of your book is equally important. Canva enables you to:

- **Create Consistent Layouts:** Design chapter headings, page numbers, and margins that provide a cohesive reading experience.

- **Incorporate Visual Elements:** Add images, illustrations, and graphics to enhance the narrative.

Publishing and Distribution

After finalizing your design, Canva allows you
to export your book in high-resolution formats
suitable for both digital and print publishing.
While Canva facilitates the design process,
you'll need to use external platforms for
distribution. Options include:

- **Amazon Kindle Direct Publishing
  (KDP):** For digital and print-on-demand
  distribution.

- **IngramSpark:** Offers wide distribution to
  bookstores and online retailers.

- **Apple Books:** For reaching readers on
  Apple devices.

Ensure you adhere to each platform's formatting and submission guidelines to guarantee a smooth publishing process.

Building a Portfolio

A well-curated portfolio is essential for showcasing your design skills to potential clients or employers. Canva provides tools to create a professional and visually appealing portfolio.

Tips for Curating Your Best Work

1. **Select Diverse Projects:** Include a range of designs that highlight your versatility and expertise in different areas.

2. **Highlight Your Strengths:** Showcase projects that reflect your unique style and technical proficiency.

3. **Provide Context:** For each project, include a brief description outlining the

objectives, your role, and the outcomes.

4. **Keep It Updated:** Regularly add new work to demonstrate ongoing development and engagement in current design trends.

Showcasing Your Portfolio Online

Canva enables you to design a digital portfolio that can be shared easily:

- **Website or Blog:** Create a personal website using platforms like WordPress or Wix, and embed your Canva designs directly.

- **PDF Portfolio:** Design a downloadable PDF that can be sent to potential clients or employers.

- **Social Media:** Share your designs on platforms like Behance, Dribbble, or

LinkedIn to reach a broader audience.

By leveraging Canva's tools, you can build a professional portfolio that effectively showcases your talents and attracts new opportunities.

Monetizing your designs with Canva is a multifaceted endeavor, encompassing

Tips, Tricks, and Best Practices

Mastering Canva involves more than just understanding its basic functionalities; it requires leveraging advanced features, staying updated with new tools, and avoiding common pitfalls. This chapter provides insights into time-saving techniques, highlights from Canva's latest updates, and strategies to ensure your designs are both effective and distinctive.

Time-Saving Techniques

Keyboard Shortcuts

Utilizing keyboard shortcuts in Canva can significantly enhance your workflow efficiency. Here are some essential shortcuts:

Basic Shortcuts:

- **Undo:** Ctrl + Z (Windows) or Command + Z (Mac)
- **Redo:** Ctrl + Y (Windows) or Command + Y (Mac)
- **Save:** Ctrl + S (Windows) or Command + S (Mac)
- **Select All:** Ctrl + A (Windows) or Command + A (Mac)

Element Shortcuts:

- **Add Text Box:** Press T
- **Add Line:** Press L
- **Add Rectangle:** Press R

- **Add Circle:** Press C

For a comprehensive list of shortcuts, refer to Canva's official help center.

Batch Editing

Batch editing allows you to apply changes to multiple elements simultaneously, streamlining the design process.

Tips for Effective Batch Editing:

- **Selecting Multiple Elements:** Hold down the Shift key and click on each element you wish to edit.
- **Grouping Elements:** After selecting, press Ctrl + G (Windows) or Command + G (Mac) to group elements, enabling collective resizing, moving, or styling.
- **Replacing Elements in Bulk:** While Canva doesn't support direct bulk replacement, you can streamline the process by using consistent naming

conventions and styles, making manual updates more efficient.

Automation Tools

Canva offers several automation features to expedite your design tasks:

- **Magic Resize:** Automatically adjust your design to fit various dimensions suitable for different platforms.
- **Brand Kit:** Store and apply your brand's colors, fonts, and logos consistently across all designs.
- **Templates:** Utilize pre-designed templates to maintain consistency and save time on repetitive projects.

Staying Up-to-Date

Canva continually evolves, introducing new features and tools to enhance user experience. Staying informed about these updates ensures you maximize the platform's potential.

Leveraging Canva's Updates

In October 2024, Canva unveiled "Droptober," a significant update introducing over 40 new features, including AI-powered tools designed to boost creativity and productivity.

Notable Additions:

- **Dream Lab:** An AI-driven image generator developed in collaboration with Leonardo.Ai, allowing users to create custom images from text descriptions.
- **Magic Write:** An enhanced AI writing assistant that offers smarter content suggestions, aiding in crafting compelling copy.
- **Interactive Charts and Polls:** Tools to create engaging, data-driven visuals and gather audience feedback in real-time.

Staying Informed:

- **Canva Newsroom:** Regularly visit Canva's newsroom for official announcements and detailed information on new features.

- **In-App Notifications:** Pay attention to in-app messages highlighting new tools and functionalities.
- **Community Forums and Blogs:** Engage with the Canva community to share insights and learn from others' experiences.

Common Pitfalls and How to Avoid Them

Even with a robust platform like Canva, designers may encounter challenges. Being aware of common pitfalls can help you navigate and overcome them effectively.

Design Mistakes

- **Overcrowded Designs:** Avoid clutter by embracing white space and focusing on essential elements.

- **Inconsistent Branding:** Utilize the Brand Kit to maintain uniformity in colors, fonts, and logos across all materials.
- **Low-Resolution Images:** Ensure all images used are high-resolution to maintain professionalism and clarity.

Technical Issues

- **Unsaved Work:** Regularly save your progress using Ctrl + S (Windows) or Command + S (Mac) to prevent data loss.
- **Browser Compatibility:** Use supported browsers and keep them updated to ensure optimal performance.
- **File Export Problems:** Double-check export settings to ensure designs are saved in the correct format and quality.

Ensuring Your Work Stands Out

- **Stay Current with Design Trends:** Regularly explore design blogs, webinars, and courses to keep your skills and knowledge up-to-date.

- **Seek Feedback:** Share your designs with peers or mentors to gain constructive insights and improve your work.
- **Experiment and Innovate:** Don't hesitate to try new tools, techniques, and ideas to push the boundaries of your creativity.

By integrating these tips, leveraging the latest features, and being mindful of common challenges, you can enhance your proficiency with Canva and produce outstanding designs that resonate with your audience.

The Future of Canva and Design Innovation

As we navigate through 2025, the realms of graphic design and digital content creation are undergoing transformative shifts. Central to this evolution are advancements in artificial intelligence (AI) and emerging technologies, which are redefining creative processes and tools. Canva, a leader in accessible design solutions, is at the forefront of this revolution, continually enhancing its platform to meet the dynamic needs of its users. This chapter delves into the emerging trends in graphic design, provides insights into Canva's roadmap, and encourages designers to embrace continuous learning and innovation.

Emerging Trends in Graphic Design

The graphic design landscape is being reshaped by several key trends, primarily driven by technological advancements and a renewed emphasis on authentic, human-centered design.

AI-Powered Design

Artificial intelligence has become an integral part of the design workflow, assisting designers in various tasks:

- **Generative Design:** AI tools can generate design elements or entire compositions based on specific inputs, offering a plethora of creative possibilities.
- **Automation of Repetitive Tasks:** Mundane tasks such as color correction,

resizing, and retouching are now streamlined through AI, allowing designers to focus more on strategic and creative aspects. citeturn0search6

- **Personalized Content Creation:** AI algorithms analyze user data to create tailored content that resonates with specific audiences, enhancing engagement and relevance.

Fusion of Analog and Digital Techniques

In response to the digital surge, there's a growing movement that celebrates human imperfection and authentic expression:

- **Analog Meets AI:** Designers are blending traditional art forms with digital enhancements, creating pieces that embody the warmth of handcrafted art and the precision of digital tools.
- **Textured Grains and Handcrafted Elements:** Incorporating tactile textures and handcrafted aesthetics adds depth and

authenticity to digital designs, appealing to audiences seeking genuine connections.

Dynamic and Interactive Branding

Brands are moving beyond static visuals to create more engaging and adaptable identities:

- **Motion Graphics:** Incorporating movement into branding elements captures attention and conveys messages more dynamically.
- **Responsive Logos:** Logos that adapt to different platforms and user interactions enhance brand versatility and user experience.
- **Interactive Design Elements:** Engaging users through interactive components fosters deeper connections and memorable brand experiences.

Canva's Roadmap

Canva is committed to staying ahead of these trends by continually evolving its platform. While specific future features are often kept under wraps until official announcements, several anticipated developments can be inferred based on industry trends and Canva's trajectory:

Advanced AI Integration

Building upon existing AI capabilities, Canva is likely to introduce more sophisticated tools:

- **Enhanced Generative Design Tools:** Allowing users to create complex visuals from simple inputs, democratizing design creation.
- **AI-Assisted Content Suggestions:** Providing real-time recommendations for design improvements and content enhancements based on project objectives.

Expansion into New Design Realms

To cater to the diverse needs of its user base, Canva may explore:

- **3D Design Capabilities:** Enabling the creation and manipulation of three-dimensional graphics within the platform.
- **Augmented Reality (AR) Design Tools:** Allowing users to design AR experiences, merging digital content with the physical world.

Enhanced Collaboration Features

Recognizing the importance of teamwork in creative projects, Canva might introduce:

- **Real-Time Multi-User Editing:** Allowing multiple users to work on a design simultaneously, enhancing collaborative efficiency.
- **Advanced Commenting and Feedback Systems:** Streamlining the review process

with threaded comments, annotations, and approval workflows.

Localization and Cultural Representation

With a global user base, Canva is poised to:

- **Expand Multilingual Support:** Offering more languages and localized templates to cater to diverse audiences.
- **Culturally Inclusive Design Assets:** Providing a broader range of templates and elements that reflect various cultural aesthetics and traditions.

Your Creative Future

In this rapidly evolving landscape, continuous learning and adaptability are paramount for designers. Here are strategies to stay ahead:

Embrace Lifelong Learning

- **Engage in Workshops and Courses:** Regularly update your skills through educational opportunities, focusing on emerging tools and techniques.
- **Participate in Design Communities:** Sharing experiences and insights with peers fosters growth and inspiration.

Experiment with New Tools

- **Explore AI and Automation:** Integrate AI tools into your workflow to enhance efficiency and open new creative avenues.
- **Adopt New Mediums:** Venturing into areas like 3D modeling, AR, or interactive design can diversify your skill set and offerings.

Focus on Authenticity

- **Develop a Unique Voice:** While tools evolve, your distinct perspective remains invaluable. Cultivate a style that reflects your individuality.

- **Prioritize Human-Centered Design:**
  Ensure that empathy and user experience
  are at the core of your creations,
  resonating on a personal level with
  audiences.

The future of design is a harmonious blend of
technological innovation and human creativity.
By staying informed, embracing new tools, and
nurturing your unique creative voice, you can
navigate and thrive in this dynamic landscape.
Canva will continue to be a steadfast partner in
your creative journey, providing the tools and
resources to bring your visions to life.

Conclusion

As you conclude this journey through the world of design with Canva, it's essential to reflect on the key lessons and insights gained, and to consider the next steps in your creative endeavors.

Reflecting on Your Journey

Throughout this book, we've explored the multifaceted capabilities of Canva, from mastering design fundamentals to leveraging advanced features for professional projects. Key takeaways include:

- **Design Fundamentals**: Understanding principles such as alignment, contrast, and hierarchy is crucial for creating visually appealing and effective designs.

- **Canva's Versatility**: Canva's extensive library of templates, elements, and tools empowers users to craft a wide range of materials, from social media graphics to educational resources.

- **Monetization Opportunities**: By creating and selling digital products or offering design services, you can transform your design skills into a sustainable income stream.

- **Community Engagement**: Participating in design communities and staying updated with Canva's latest features fosters continuous learning and inspiration.

Remember, design is an evolving field. Embrace experimentation, seek inspiration from diverse sources, and continually refine your skills to stay ahead of trends.

Next Steps

With the knowledge and skills acquired, consider the following actions to further your design journey:

1. **Apply Your Skills**: Start by creating designs for personal projects, local businesses, or community events to gain practical experience.

2. **Join the Canva Creators Community**: Engage with a global network of designers by becoming a Canva Creator. This platform allows you to share your designs, receive feedback, and even earn royalties based on your content's performance.

3. **Stay Informed**: Regularly visit the Canva Design School for tutorials, design inspiration, and updates on new features.

4. **Participate in Design Challenges**: Engage in design challenges to test your creativity, receive constructive feedback, and connect with other designers.

5. **Explore Advanced Features**: Delve into Canva's advanced tools, such as Magic Studio, to enhance your designs with AI-powered features.

6. **Build a Portfolio**: Create an online portfolio showcasing your best work to attract potential clients or employers.

7. **Seek Feedback**: Join design communities to share your work, receive feedback, and learn from others.

8. **Keep Learning**: Design trends and tools are continually evolving. Commit to lifelong learning to stay relevant in the field.

By taking these steps, you can apply what you've learned, connect with a global community of Canva creators, and continue to grow and innovate in your design career.

www.ingramcontent.com/pod-product-compliance
Lightning Source LLC
LaVergne TN
LVHW052124070326
832902LV00038B/3647